Celebrate Win...

All About
Snowmen

by Kathryn Clay

raintree
a Capstone company — publishers for children

Raintree is an imprint of Capstone Global Library Limited, a company incorporated in England and Wales
having its registered office at 7 Pilgrim Street, London, EC4V 6LB – Registered company number: 6695582

www.raintree.co.uk
myorders@raintree.co.uk

Text © Capstone Global Library Limited 2016
The moral rights of the proprietor have been asserted.

Edited by Erika L. Shores
Designed by Cynthia Della-Rovere
Picture research by Tracy Cummins
Production by Tori Abraham

Printed and bound in China.

ISBN 978 1 4747 0311 6
19 18 17 16 15
10 9 8 7 6 5 4 3 2 1

British Library Cataloguing in Publication Data
A full catalogue record for this book is available from the British Library.

Acknowledgements
Getty Images: Blend Images/Don Maso, 21; iStockphoto: FrankyDeMeyer, 19, Marilyn Nieves, 5, studio9400, 9;
Shutterstock: Brykaylo Yuriy, 13, KPG_Payless, 15, PRILL, 3, sellingpix, Design Element, Smit, Cover, Suzanne
Tucker, 1, Vivid Pixels, 17, wizdata, 11; Thinkstock: Pavel Losevsky, 7.

Contents

Winter fun

Winter is here!

Snow is falling.

Let's build some snowmen.

Choose the right snow.

Dry snow won't stay together.

Sticky snow works best.

Build a body

Make a body first.
Pack the snow
into a snowball.

Roll the ball along the ground.

Snow sticks to the snowball.

The ball gets bigger.

Make another ball.

This is the snowman's middle.

Make a smaller ball.

This is the snowman's head.

The snowman needs arms.
Two sticks will work.

Funny face

Time to add eyes
and buttons.
Dan uses rocks.

The snowman needs a nose.
Maddy uses a carrot.

Dressing up

Emma's snowman has a scarf.
She adds a purple hat.

How will you dress
your snowman?

Glossary

button round object used to fasten clothing

pack push together tightly

scarf length of fabric worn around the neck

snowball ball of packed snow

winter one of the four seasons of the year; winter comes after autumn and before spring

Read more

What Can Live in the Snow? (What Can Live There?), John-Paul Wilkins (Raintree, 2014)

What Can You See in Winter? (Seasons), Sian Smith (Raintree, 2014)

Websites

www.naturedetectives.org.uk/winter/
Download winter wildlife ID sheets, pick up some great snowy-weather-game ideas and discover all the fun you can have with winter sticks!

www.wildlifewatch.org.uk/
Explore the Wildlife Trust's wildlife watch website and get busy this winter spotting interesting winter plants and animals living near by! Follow badger's blog for great wildlife spotting tips and some fascinating photographs.

Index